ADDICTED

to

FEAR

MY JOURNEY TO FREEDOM

PATRICE Y. AMBROISE

ISBN 978-1-0980-3430-6 (paperback)
ISBN 978-1-0980-3431-3 (digital)

Copyright © 2020 by Patrice Y. Ambroise

All rights reserved. No part of this publication may be reproduced, distributed, or transmitted in any form or by any means, including photocopying, recording, or other electronic or mechanical methods without the prior written permission of the publisher. For permission requests, solicit the publisher via the address below.

Christian Faith Publishing, Inc.
832 Park Avenue
Meadville, PA 16335
www.christianfaithpublishing.com

Printed in the United States of America

I dedicate this book to my sweet little grandson Vaury Alexander Drew Damas, whom we lost this past year. Vaury, you have given me more determination in my life to be who God has designed me to be. With just an hour of breath, you have changed my world forever. I love you beyond explanation and am determined to live and not just exist every day I am granted. Until I hold you again in my arms, I will continue to hold you in my heart. You will always be my sweet little boy. I love you!

CONTENTS

ACKNOWLEDGMENT

Thank you to my husband, Drew, I love being your rib. I thank God for designing you for me and me for you. Doing life with you is a treasure that I hold dear to my heart every day. To my wonderful children Jazmyne, J'anelle, Jordin, Jehna, and Jeyden, precious grandchildren Avryanna, Zyair, and Leyanna, you are all such a blessing to me. Thank you for trusting and believing in me. To my father, Melvin, thank you for loving me, supporting me, and pouring into me every day of my life. I love being a daddy's girl. Last but not least, to my mother and Proverbs 39 woman, Denise, you have taught me how to draw near to God, love with everything I have, and press into who God created me to be. I love you and am beyond grateful to call you mom. You all are simply the most amazing gifts from God and I thank you for being a part of my world.

START RIGHT HERE

Before we begin to peel back the layers, we must first understand the difference between fear and reverence. We find that when reading the Bible, we are told to fear God and yet we are also told God did not give us the spirit of fear. How can this be? Are we supposed to have fear for God and not have fear at the same time? Absolutely not. When the Bible speaks about the "spirit of fear," it is referring to the spirit that brings about emotions connected to harm, horror, distress, and panic for example.

When the Bible refers to the "fear of God," it speaks to reverence. To revere God is to show a deep respect for him. To honor him and acknowledge his sovereignty. It is not speaking of us being afraid of a big bad god who looks only to punish us or to press us down. When we (fear) revere God, we respect, admire, and adore the living God who created us and loves us.

We often make the mistake of confusing humility with humiliation as well. When we humble ourselves, we recognize and have a modest view of ourselves compared to God. Lacking any vanity, whereas humiliation is the feeling or notion of being embarrassed, ashamed, or dishonored. Recognizing that God is God in every way and honoring him is not the same as belittling ourselves before him as if he is an unreasonable and unattainable God. God doesn't want us to dishonor ourselves to claim that He is Lord. He wants us to recognize who He is and who we are in him, so we can live a life covered in His grace and mercy and wrapped in His love.

Being clear about the terms and actions we use toward ourselves, others, and especially God is important. Be sure to research what you don't understand so that you can always make clear decisions about the things you hear, learn, or experience.

Now let's get started.

CHAPTER 1

The Day of Discovery

Tears had been flowing uncontrollably for months. Whether I was at home, at work, cooking dinner, or even driving my kids to school, they would just begin to flow. I began to suffer from anxiety attacks as well. After scheduling an appointment with my doctor, he prescribed me something for the anxiety and he also told me, "No, you are not going through the change," which was my own diagnosis. I tried to continue with my days, until the final attack happened.

While shopping at the mall, I was trying to decide what to buy for myself (key word: MYSELF) when I began to feel overwhelmed. My chest began to tighten, and my heart and thoughts began to race. Before this moment, I had not taken any of the prescribed medication because I'm not a fan of any medications. I don't like foreign things in my body or the lack of control (key word: CONTROL). But I took one quickly, as I found myself in tears inside of the store.

The medicine took effect rapidly and before I knew it, I was drowsy while driving and begging God to get me home safely. This is when I knew I needed help for sure. I scheduled an appointment with a psychologist in my town and off I went on a journey I had no clue that I was already on. Boy, I was not ready, or so I thought.

As I sat in the doctor's office, pouring out the pain and confusion over the last few months, I had a moment of clarity as he asked me this question: "What was it like when you were a child?" Ouch! It went something like this.

When I was five this happened, at ten this happened, and the list continued on and on recanting from birth to the present age. Story after story, trauma after trauma, I had survived them all, even felt victorious and not just a victim anymore. But what I had not done was completely deal with them all.

Every part of me had been infected by the pain and confusion that I had experienced and so desperately tried to push beneath the surface. I hadn't cried for the molested child or the homeless teenager. I hadn't mourned the loss of peace, innocence, or joy that was continuously snatched from my life. It's ironic how now thinking about it, I feel bad for that little girl who continued to suffer in silence.

As time grew to a close with the doctor, the floodgates were open, and I now had to go home. When I walked into the house, one of my older daughters and my cousin were sitting in the living room staring at my swollen red face. With great concern, they asked me "What's wrong?" and "What can we do?" I asked them to leave the house and give me some time alone. I knew whatever was bleeding out of the surface needed no witnesses and was beyond natural help. I could not be touched. So I quickly went straight upstairs to my room before they could hug me.

It was there in my bed, as I scratched at my skin, I realized I had an addiction. I had been afraid my whole life. The fear of expressing myself was hidden behind self-erected walls. With tears racing down my face, the sounds of a wounded animal were blaring past my lips and I could not control the urge to get out of my own skin. It felt like it wasn't a part of me, as if I was wrapped in a dirty cloth and I was disgusted. In this moment, all the movies I had seen where people went through recovery and suffered through those first few weeks of withdrawal came rushing through my brain. There were tears, sweat, and a whole lot of pain and agony pouring out of me.

How could this be? I hadn't done drugs or alcohol. How could I be going through these same motions and emotions of an addict? How, I asked? Simply stated, something was in me that didn't belong to me, and I was continuously taking part in it day after day.

That day I cried until my eyes ran out of tears and my body was too weak to scream any more. From the bed to the floor and back to the bed again over and over again, I was emotionally and physically tapped out. When I think back, I can see how I wasn't trying to cry out to God; rather, I was simply crying out my pain. All that which was held captive in me was beginning to explode out of me like a volcano erupting. Finally, a sense of peace came over me and then I slept. I had been through enough for one day. But I knew it was far from over.

Questions to Ask Yourself

1. Do you suffer from anxiety?

2. Do you cry without reason?

3. Do you shake off your tears but don't deal with the pain?

Pray This Prayer with Me

Lord, as I find myself engaged in this journey, help me to see myself through Your eyes. Show me the areas that are affected by this thing called fear. Reveal to me the places where I have hidden pain and how I react from these places. Give me the strength and courage I need for this journey as I push into the place of healing. Thank You for guiding me and healing me and staying with me always. In Jesus' name, amen.

CHAPTER 2

Lights On

I love to go walking. It is supposed to be for exercise, but I enjoy the peace of it. On my walks, I can hear from God so clearly. It truly is a peaceful moment, my own Garden of Eden. But before we get too tranquil, let me tell you it is also the place where God corrects me and guides me. This particular day, I was so unprepared for the level of revelation and light I was about to receive.

I headed out as I usually do but something led me to go a different route. It is a shorter route and well on this day my legs wouldn't have been able to make it through the longer route I was used to. The Lord had chosen this day to shine light upon my true relationship with fear, and it was not pretty.

He said this to me: "Fear is attached to you. It started when you were very young and has grown with you." He shared that it used to provoke me, to control me, but now I go looking for it. What appeared next was surprising to say the least. My jaw was so wide open, it seemed to be hanging on the ground.

There beside me appeared a form no larger than my torso and it had a rope that went in and out of it and me. We were tied together in different parts of our bodies like we were laced up together. I was shocked at our connection and even more that I could feel the ties.

God said to me, "See? You engage it now even when it does not engage you." There I was with visions of me pulling on the strings to see if it was still there, if it still hurt, and if we were still connected. That may seem like I was working through deliverance, but instead I was assuring myself that I was still connected to it. Ouch!

It was like having a toothache that stopped hurting, so you push on it to see if it is still irritated or in pain. Not that you want it to be, but you are curious because you have not thought about it and it hasn't been bothering you.

The Lord then said to me, "You have been trained and have accepted its lifestyle. It no longer needs to harass you daily or make itself known to you. You now search it out to see if it's still there for you." Double ouch!

As I cut down another street, the Lord began to show me how I had used fear instead of wisdom and faith. It was a lifetime of believing that if I was afraid of something, more than likely that wasn't for me. Even if I tried to continue to move forward, I would be searching and wondering when the floor would drop out beneath me. I would think things like, *Don't go out with your husband tonight, you may need money for milk in the morning; Don't be who you are, others may not like you or worse believe you love Jesus; Don't buy yourself anything, you could use that money to buy something for someone else, or someone may need something. What if something happens, you could have used the money for that? But what if you did purchase something, then you would spend every moment blaming yourself for getting it.*

Fear disguises itself as many things, one of which is wisdom. It makes you believe that what you are really operating in is wisdom. "You are more mature for your age" and "wise beyond your years" are some of the other comments you will believe. While this may be true in some cases, most of the time fear is giving you reasons to not try new things, to not make changes, or to not press forward in a particular area. It is less embarrassing to say I just don't believe I should/could/would do it, instead of "I am afraid, embarrassed, or ashamed to try." "For God did not give us the spirit of timidity (fear), but a spirit of power, of love, and of self-discipline (Sound mind)" (2 Timothy 1:7). Are you fearful at your core where no one else can see? Do you feel powerful and loving? Do you have a sound mind?

Questions to Ask Yourself

1. What is your true relationship with fear?

2. Where does fear end and you begin?

3. Have you been searching for opportunities to use fear instead of faith?

4. Ask God to continue to open your eyes to how much you are involved with fear.

Pray This Prayer with Me

Lord, I come to You today with a repentant heart ready to surrender fear and turn the other way. I have spent so much time in a relationship with fear more concerned and focused on it and not you. Forgive me for holding on to the chains that have kept me bound to fear instead of trusting in the freedom I have in You. Thank You for shedding light on this relationship and the ways I have fostered it throughout the years. My eyes are open to see the truth, my heart is ready to receive You as Lord, and my ears are ready to receive your direction and your correction. Guide me through this as I give You thanksgiving and praise. In Jesus' name, amen.

CHAPTER 3

Whose Hand Are You Holding?

The walk seemed to have taken just moments but was filled with a lifetime of explanations. As you can see, I felt the need to break it up into a couple of chapters so that you too can break down the moments and revelations you will encounter.

So, there I was, tied together with fear, using it as my source of "wisdom." It felt like a hammer dropped on my heart. I had barely grasped that moment when the Lord then showed me my relationship with him. I was so shocked and heartbroken, but yet I totally understood and was extremely saddened by my actions. I had let fear become my master even in my relationship with the Father.

As I stood on the side of the street, my hand out holding onto fear, I asked it to join hands with the Lord on my behalf. (That's right my jaw dropped too.) I will say it again. I was holding fear's hand and asking fear's other hand to connect to God. It was as if my desire for a relationship with God was filtered through my relationship with fear. How could this make sense and why?

The Lord began to share with me that even in my interactions with Him throughout the years, fear had been there all along. I had never truly let God all the way in. He was subject to the fear I held on to and could only come as far as the boundaries and walls I had created in fear. Though I was connected to and loved God, I was limited in my interactions with Him and the fullness I could receive from him because of my relationship with fear.

I was not operating as a bride of Christ in true intimacy. There is a horrible saying that goes, "a girlfriend with a wife on the side." Sounds crazy, right? Except that's what the reality was. I had "fear" with some God on the side. Even though God is the constant faithful, loving, gracious, merciful God, I had not placed him before everything else and fear had taken up residency in my heart.

This is a big pill to swallow, but we must recognize the raw, exposed truth of what we are dealing with and where we are. In our nakedness, we can only see where all the marks and curvatures are in our being. Fear is a spirit and God is a Spirit (*the* Spirit), so how can your spirit be in a committed relationship with both? The book of Matthew 6:24 references the love of money and the love of God and not being able to serve both. It is the same in every relationship. You cannot serve fear and serve God. There is just no way. You will love one and hate the other. I know it is unfathomable to think of saying I hate God. We don't hate him, but when we allow fear to be on the throne of our hearts, we are treating him as such.

Do we use God's definition of love for our relationship with him? We can say we would never hate God, that's so extreme, yet we would dishonor Him by trying to be in a relationship with Him and fear. Anything you submit to, meditate on, and live by is your god. Yet the first commandment is one God and no one before Him.

These words are not to beat you up. You've already been doing that too much. This is to bring revelation and to shine light upon what has been kept in the darkness. The enemy and his kind don't care if you sing in the choir, talk about God, or are just a regular good old person. *He Absolutely Does Not Care!* Nope, he cares whom you serve, sit with, understand, and are obedient to. So, in this journey, when the days get hard, remind yourself that you are fighting for freedom (your own first). Picture yourself submitted and walking in the enemy's army (I know this would never happen). Now picture yourself with chains on but walking ahead of your commander, "fear," because he has you so trained you are off to the races for him.

This is reality, folks. Until you break that spirit off of you, this is what you look like. How many believers are on that side of the fence and don't even know it? Our God owns cattle on a thousand hills, but we live in fear of eating. He has given us dominion over the earth, yet we walk around as paupers and slaves. Peace is ours for the taking, and boldness is in our DNA. We are victorious yet and still our minds race with defeating thoughts. We shy away from most things and see ourselves failing or as failures most of the time.

Even our decisions about how to worship God are clouded by saying, "I don't want to be over the top, did I shout too loud?" or "I am the worst at fasting and I don't know enough of the word to speak." At the end of the day, all God desires is a true relationship with him.

Let me be clear: Discovering that you are in a relationship with fear is not a determination on whether you love God but rather it's a clarity on how you let him love you. There has been a breach of God's space. Those born addicted and those who have sought it out still have to go through the withdrawal all the same. So there is no sense of getting caught up in the emotions of would've, should've, could've when you have work to do. Amen.

Questions to Ask Yourself

1. Is fear a part of your relationship with God?

2. Who drives your thoughts and actions?

3. What kind of bride are you? (Remember, men, this is the "Word," not just a reference to the females. The church is the bride of Christ.)

4. Is fear your main source with God on the side?

5. Are you ready to realign?

Pray This Prayer with Me

Father (Abba), I Thank You for this day of revelation. Although it is painful to realize that I have kept you out of areas of my life, I am so grateful you have shown me the light of these situations. Forgive me, Lord, for every moment I spent holding on to fear's hand instead of your hand. Forgive me for not allowing You in but instead being upset that I could not receive You in fullness. Forgive me for turning to fear instead of turning to You in faith, believing in who You are and what You have directed me to do. I repent, Lord. I Thank You for Your forgiveness and this new start to my monogamist relationship with You. I love You, Lord. Teach me how to receive Your love, in Jesus' name, amen.

Guiding Thoughts

Now that you have repented, you need to divorce fear. So write out your divorce decree and sign it. Remember to make it personal to you. Remember that you never signed a prenuptial agreement, so get all your stuff back. Your strength, boldness, joy, freedom, peace, and so on and so on. Today is going to be a draining day at first but also a day of empowerment. So be courageous and move forward.

CHAPTER 4

Pity Party, Table for One

Pity Party? No one has time for that. Now that you can see clearer, you may become frustrated with yourself or feel this pressure to make up for time that has passed. Well, you don't have time for a pity party or anything that resembles it. While you do have work ahead of you, the good thing is that you know it and you are still here to get it done.

So today shake off everything that will try to steal your joy and enjoy a good deep breath. We are going to start today off with a good thought. What does God say about me? Psalm 139:14 tells you that "you are fearfully and wonderfully made." I know you may be thinking that is great and all, but let's get moving to the deliverance. Just join me for a bit.

In Genesis chapter 1, when God created the earth and all its workings before He made man, He saw it and said "It is good," but after he created us (Adam and Eve) and gave Earth over to them, "He saw that it was very good." It is no happening chance the wording was different after man was created. You, my dear, God sees as very good. Hebrews 2:6 says, "What is man that you are mindful of him, son of man that you care for him?" Our Father thinks about us! He is mindful of us. Mindful is defined as conscious or aware of something.

We are not an afterthought. You are not an afterthought. You have a designated space in his thought processes. *You matter to God,* not just in what you will do but just because He loves you. So don't get stuck in a pity party because this is where fear wants to distract you. Like an old lover you just broke up with, it will send out feelers to see if it can still hold your attention or get an emotional reaction out of you.

Case in point: They send you a text message.

Fear: I love you.

You: No response.

Fear: Remember when _____

You: I don't want to talk about that.

Guess what? You just engaged it and you are back on the hook. Do not respond unless it is with the Word of God. When you repent, let it go, God has it. Anything that chooses to keep you feeling sorry or bad about yourself is not of God. Repentance comes with a change of heart, not with a hammer to beat yourself up with. Ownership of what you've done or where you've been comes with an open door of where you are going.

So why all the scriptures of what God thinks of you? Simply stated, this is who you are and were created to be. This should also give you a road map of where you are going. Before you clean out the moldy basement, you might want to put on a mask and some gloves. The dust will fly and a mess will be made before you sort through it all. Keep what you need and toss what is causing the mold, dust, clutter, and confusion. By preparing yourself with the Word, you will find that as you tear back the layers and open the boxes of your past, you may cough but you won't collapse. Putting on the Word is like putting on protective gear. It keeps you safe from all that could cause harm or damage to you. So get ready and get prepared.

Questions to Ask Yourself

1. Make a list of scriptures of what God thinks about you.

    (I have added a few in the back of the book to get you started.)

2. Make a list of God's characteristics and attributes and keep them both handy.

    Use them daily. Start off by using one of each answer daily. Use them to remind you of who God says you are when thoughts come up to tear you down. Then remind yourself of who He is that His word is greater than any thoughts or words that have been spoken against you. Now, breathe!

Pray This Prayer with Me

Dear Lord, I Thank You for your love and faithfulness, for creating me, and for being mindful of me. Today I choose to see myself through Your eyes, and I truly receive Your forgiveness into my heart. In the name of Jesus, I release myself from my past and am now standing in a place of excitement for the future I have in You. Lord, for any day that I feel burdened down or downcast, please bring quickly to my remembrance all that I have and all that I am in You. Lord, Thank You for never leaving me or forsaking me. I love You, Lord! In the name of Jesus, amen.

CHAPTER 5

I Want to Be in Control

It was the spring of 2007 and I needed major back surgery. I had ruptured two discs, L4 and L5, and I was losing mobility in my legs. (I found out, after surgery, I had only about two weeks left before I would have been paralyzed from the waist down.) I was facing such a huge decision to have the surgery two weeks before the recital of the studio I own. During an emotional conversation, one of my best friends told me I was a control freak. *What? How rude!* Right? I was so offended. I was not a control freak, but wait a minute, let me give you a couple of examples and you can decide.

Delegating is not one of my strong suits. I'm more of the do-it-yourself kind of person. Anyone else with me? It's just easier to do it by yourself than to worry that it won't get done or it won't get done right. Okay, now some hands should be flying in the air while screaming "That's me." Here I was facing back surgery one week before my recital, which spells out no dancing, minimal movement, and yes, needing help. *Aaahhh!* So there I was, with not really a decision, but hoping it was. Do the surgery now or wait. I gave the doctor my "laminated" plan on how this should play out. First, I would do my recital, I had another surgery planned already, so I would do that next and then I would do the back surgery. Well, the doctor said, "If I develop a condition referred to as clap foot, I would never dance again." So off I went to the operating room. My control of the situation was out of the window and I wasn't too thrilled about it either.

Here is another great example of how fear can operate in your life through control. Many times, my husband has offered to help out with the business portion of my studio, and many times I have said yes. But, just as many times I have retracted my yes without saying no, I would just begin to do the work for myself again. It was never about him but rather my own fears—fears that he could see me struggling, stumbling, even falling down (failing). My thoughts were, *If I do it all myself and fix it, he won't see it and he won't think less of me.* Well, that flawed logic went out the window during one birthday dinner when he shed light on the truth of the situation.

There we were out on the town after a lovely lobster dinner. We were discussing the studio and I finally shared my yo-yo issue with the business. I shared how I didn't want him to see the bad stuff or me struggling, and then it happened. He smiled and said so sweetly, "Babe, you don't think I can see you?" *Pow!* What a revelation. Of course, he could see me and you know what? So could God. We continued our conversation as we walked around, and it actually was a relief to know that I didn't feel the need to hide in plain sight anymore.

We hold onto control in hopes no one, especially God, won't see us fail. Even though we know He sees all, we try to fix it before going to Him or in the middle of going to Him because we take on shame and doubt that the enemy gives us or we place on ourselves.

Our need to control things no matter what the issue or circumstance comes from one place: fear! During my surgery, it was fear that the recital couldn't go on without me and I would appear weak and people wouldn't want to come back. With my husband, there was embarrassment, even though we are living out this life together and of course he can see me struggling. Fear leads us to a desire to control things with the assumption that we won't be exposed. We buy the lie that we need to take everything under our wing, both good and bad. Let me ask you this: Would you rather take responsibility for something failing than to ask for help? Are you looking to accomplish something so others can see you have value? That is fear.

Remember, fear comes in many disguises. A big one is "control." I had always believed a control freak was someone who tried to control others in a negative or abusive way, which it still is for some people. But now you can see that being a controlling person can come from fear of getting hurt or being embarrassed or shamed as well. I wasn't trying to harm anyone else. I was trying to protect myself.

As a mother, wife, daughter, sister, grandmother, aunt, friend, leader, and teacher, my days are filled with trying to fix it. I want to help. I don't want anyone to be hurt or sad. So I add to my day with comments like, of course, "I can do it," "My day is already packed, but what is one more thing, right?" "Wouldn't want anyone to be disappointed, right?" Truly the list never ends, but where is God in your desire to handle everything. How is He in control if you are too?

Today has been filled with questions you need to ask yourself and evaluations of your true intentions. Don't skip over them. Be completely honest with yourself about the root and the source of the things that you find.

Questions to Ask Yourself

1. How many things are you in control of?

2. If you weren't around, what do you fear would come to pass?

    (Don't freak out, God still would be God and the world would still go on)

3. What if you didn't get to control things during your day, what would you do? How would you feel?

Pray This Prayer with Me

Lord, Thank You for my journey to freedom and the continued revelation day by day. Forgive me for every moment I have stood in Your way and operated in fear through control. Help me to relinquish control to You day by day. I desire to rest in You and be at peace with Your plan. I love You, Lord. In Jesus' name, amen.

CHAPTER 6

Where Did I Get This?

Control comes from fear and fear grows in our need to control. Fear controls control. Before we can articulate fear, it begins to train us. Those around us play a huge part in where it originates from and how and whether it grows and grows.

Let's get started by taking a brief stroll down memory lane. Follow me. At the age five, I received my first kiss from a boy and he smacked me right after. Seems regular, right? Not really. This is also the year I began to be molested, which continued throughout my elementary years. This was also the year we began moving from town to town, that I can remember. I went to eight schools by tenth grade, homeless at age fourteen, had my first daughter at age fifteen, followed by my second daughter at age sixteen, and had been engaged and unengaged while graduating high school by age seventeen. Don't get me wrong, there were some amazing things happening as well. But my home was always filled with chaos, arguing, uncertainties, and buckets of love. Yup, the last one threw you and me too.

I had more love from my parents than some even know to hope for, but life was always crazy. I have always been the apple of my parent's eyes, but I've also always carried the weight of peacemaker too. Nothing in my life was ever certain, except their love for me.

At dinner, just a few years ago, my husband Drew and I were talking about some of my moves, like waking up at a friend's house to go home and finding when I got there that I didn't have one anymore. My husband looked at me with sadness and said, "This explains so much. Now I see why you always seem to expect the worse or look for what may come next." My first thoughts were, *It's been like twenty years, dude, and you've heard these stories before,* but then I realized my own light bulb went off too. I grew up in fear and had been taught without words that nothing in life is dependable or certain, not even the ones you love or who love you.

I had no grasp on what living in peace looked like on an extended basis, and I surely had no true expectations of its possibilities. Rather I was a girl gripped by fear and trying to take hold of life by controlling it. Sadly, that isn't even possible, yet so many of us believe in its (phantom) strength.

Control seems to give us a sense of strength and stability. Holding onto every exit strategy, planning for every possibility, or just having your hand in every situation gives you a sense of peace. But trust me, it is no comparison to the real thing.

There is no true peace in being in control because simply stated, God's not in it. The word tells us in Philippians 4:6–7: Do not be anxious about anything, but in everything, by prayer and petition, with thanksgiving, present your requests to God. And the peace of God which transcends all understanding will guard your hearts and your minds in Christ Jesus.

Just imagine taking your ball of nerves and packing them up and handing them over, saying, "Thanks, God, I'm going to enjoy an uninterrupted moment of _____ (you fill in the blank) while you handle this stress, worry or anxiety."

Being in control of things when you are standing in the way of God will keep you dealing with the spirit of fear and anxiety. It is not possible for you to live on the throne of your heart and God live there too. We must also grapple with the fact that fear is lack of faith and lack of faith makes us grab hold of control for dear life. Yet life was created to be lived with a reverence to God so that we can enjoy the peace and freedom that comes with that relationship. Find in yourself the truth about your need to be in control at all times.

Questions to Ask Yourself

1. Can you delegate?

2. If you can, how does that make you feel?

3. How many days this past week did you feel stressed or anxious?

4. Did you pray first or try to work out your own situations with your own solutions?

Pray This Prayer with Me

Father, I Thank You that I don't need to be in control. You made the heavens and the earth and are more than capable of handling every situation in my life. I surrender to You knowing that it is only You who can handle all my life and the lives of my loved ones with your perfect care. Thank You for being patient with me when I got in your way and tried to play god and forgive me for believing I could do it all by myself. Lord, I give it all to You. In Jesus' name, amen.

CHAPTER 7

Gathering Your Fears

Today should be exciting for all of my planners, yet the title may have turned your stomach a little bit. Taking an account of all the places that hold you captive will help you discern where to go to next and what to tear down.

No one likes to admit what they are truly afraid of except when it's a surface fear. For example, if you don't like snakes, like me, you don't have a problem shouting it from the mountaintops. But hold on a minute. What if your greatest fear is not being in control or of being abandoned? What then? Are you prepared to shout that out from the mountaintop?

I was going through a particularly difficult time in my life and begging God to help me. (Note: When you beg, you are prone not to hear because you are doing so much talking, crying, and complaining. Oh, and yes, pleading.) During this time, I was digging for any scripture to bring me peace and clarity. To my surprise, a scripture I knew became a sledgehammer against my greatest fears—a fear I didn't know I had until this moment.

Joshua 1:6 states, "I will never leave you or forsake you." I have heard a lot of preachers use this scripture in the past, but this time was different. I researched *forsake* and the tears began to flow when

I put it all together. To forsake means to abandon, renounce, or to give up.

I had a huge abandonment issue. I was so in pain from feeling so lonely, I couldn't help but stand in the gap to try to stop any more pain or afflictions that were coming my way. I had grown up around people but never really felt connected. My family had love, but the constant chaos made it apparent that I could be alone with the world on my shoulders, while in a room with a ton of people sitting around me.

Fears *disguised* themselves (there goes that word again), they hide themselves. Isn't it easier to swallow being in control than to admit you are afraid of what may happen or be lost if you aren't in control? What are your deepest fears? Can you trace the lines back to some of the sources? Today I want you to really take your time (even in private) to answer all these questions both throughout the reading and below. Ask God to uncover that which has been hiding deep down with in you all this time.

Questions to Ask Yourself

1. Take account of your fears.

2. Write down things you believe are concerns that keep you closed off and disconnected from others.

Pray This Prayer with Me

Father, Thank You for this process. Help me to face the truth of what's behind my addiction to fear. Show me how I got into this relationship and allowed it to grow. Abba (Daddy), I need You to hold me tighter as some of these answers may cause me pain. I need You, and I Thank You for revelation. In Jesus' name, Amen, Amen, Amen.

CHAPTER 8

Peeling Back the Layers

"No one will be able to stand against you all the days of your life. As I was with Moses, so I will be with you; I will never leave you nor forsake you" (Joshua 1:5). This is a promise we must learn to receive. (Please take time to read the first chapter of Joshua.)

When you peel an onion, you will find that the closer you get to the center, the more pronounced the smell is. In everything, the source of what it is, is at its core. Finding the core to your fear is key. My fear of abandonment, change, or loss goes all the way back to kindergarten (actually before, but this is where a huge staple comes in for me).

When I was five years old, my parents divorced. What should have been the closing to this crazy door actually was an opening to the amusement park, as I like to call it. There were few days when it was like a merry-go-round, but most months and years were filled with wild spinning rides, looping roller coasters, and ginormous drops. No wonder the swings are my favorite ride. They are consistent. They take you up above everything and everyone and as you look out at your surroundings, the breeze feels wonderful. But even up there, you must focus and not lean back or you may fall.

It doesn't matter what ride you are on; you must trust that it will hold you and not break down. Well, things in my life were broken. Although I was strapped in with love, I was still hanging upside down.

Even though the divorce was final, my dad still wanted to be with his family. Lots of things transpired, and he and my mother were on and off again for almost ten years. We (my mother, brother, and I) would move to get away and he would follow. Or they would come together and he would move us someplace new. This went on from first grade through tenth grade and through eight different schools. I lived on a bus fleeing one state which lasted seven days. While staying at a friend's house, my home was packed up and moved to a new house without warning. We just came home and everything was gone. That day my mom, brother, and I became homeless. After living that way for months, I decided to leave my mom's side (my best friend) for the first time in my life just to gain some sense of normalcy. This only added to my confusion, loss, and abandonment of security. It was beyond painful, and this is just a mere portion of my life's events.

In the midst of every moment of my life till this day, I have had the most loving, generous, supportive, and encouraging parents ever. They love me beyond explanation. Yup! Confusing, considering the last paragraph. How could so much love and so much pain and confusion coexist?

At one point, my dad did leave when I was older, via a phone call, and I was living with him at that time. But that wasn't the abandonment/forsaken moment. It was just a drop in the very large pot of confusion. I have never been sure of what the day would bring. Was there going to be war in the house? Would we move in the midnight hour, or would it be just a "normal" day of school and dance? When you don't learn to trust, you learn not to trust. If you don't have faith to believe, then more than likely you have been operating in fear of what may happen.

We often do a few things with our past experiences. We lump them in one pile together to add up what has happened, whether good or bad (usually the bad), or we try to shove them in a virtual closet and pretend they don't exist. Funny thing is both of these actions are for show because under the surface, we are still dealing with, reacting to, and working from these experiences—except we are unaware that we are.

All/most of my reactions and decisions were affected by my past. Although I was doing my best in each passing moment, the truth is the layer people saw was only a covering to what was underneath. It's time to peel away at the surface and discover your action source.

Questions to Ask Yourself

1. Choose one (fear, concern, anxiety) at a time and trace the source of it

2. Take the time to release your pain over those you are prepared to deal with.

3. Write about them.

4. Share with confidence.

5. Cry, scream into a pillow, and be free in the emotion that comes with it.

6. Pray out to God with pure honesty about your frustrations, fears, pain, agony, disappointments. (Remember, in order to be made whole, you must be transparent and honest.)

Pray This Prayer with Me

Lord, Thank You for the discovery of the source of my participation with fear. I Thank You in the midst of the peeling process. I

know as I uncover the things left in darkness, light will surely come. Father, bring to my remembrance things I have locked away so I can surrender them to You. Give me boldness to face the reality of where I have come from and what I have gone through. Lord, I need you in every area in my life; I welcome You in. Thank You for meeting my needs. In the precious name of Jesus, amen.

CHAPTER 9

Empowered to Choose

You need sharp tools to grind down into the roots to do away with them completely. This is a job for your sword. You must learn to encourage yourself. At first glance, you may think this means with general words you have heard from others or even used yourself. But no! If you have layers of an infection, a topical cream just won't cut it. You need a solid life-giving antidote for your spirit that is also death to the virus. I know, this sounds wildly impossible, but it is exactly what the Word of God is for.

Ephesians 6:16–17 says, "In addition to all this, take up the shield of faith, with which you can extinguish all the flaming arrows of the evil one, Take the helmet of salvation and the sword of the Spirit, which is the word of God." (Please always read above and below scriptures, but for the sake of time this will be our focus.) So you have your faith to extinguish the attacks of the enemy and your sword to cut it down. I feel encouraged when I find directions and clarity to help better my life and situations.

So when encountering your memories, attitudes, thoughts, actions, and even others who come against the Word of God on your life, you must be prepared to use the tools you have been given. *Low self-esteem really boils down to a lack of knowledge of who you are.* If you truly grasped your worth, you would not have to or even dare to entertain such self-deprecating thoughts. We struggle too often with lack of knowledge because what knowledge we do have we do not put into action. Yup, that hurts! But it is real. We must act on what we learn. Knowing is just the beginning of the battle; we must discover what the rest is and take action. *Selah* (def. pause and reflect).

Even when our life doesn't seem to align with what God says about us, we are faced with an opportunity to choose. Choose the report of your Creator who will redeem you to Himself or choose the report of your past, others, or even your own faltered state of reality. You must make a choice of what and who your faith will lie in.

My mother always says, "Sometimes it is so hard to receive or even understand God's love because it's so good, too good." This can be so true. So many believers are okay with wanting to serve God but are too afraid that they are unworthy to receive His grace or, even worse, that He may take it all back. I mean, he has the right to withhold anything, even love. Except it is not in His nature or character, and He would never go against His own character. While sometimes we may think it's not possible, we say things like, "This is who I am, everyone I came from is like this and so on and so on." The explanations of why not could continue on for miles if we write them down. But what if God's Word was true? What if by using His Word and definition of who we are, we could get rid of those haunting, belittling, degrading comments that circle around in our heads? By being transformed by the renewing of your minds.

Two things cannot occupy the same space at the same time. If you are constantly thinking negative things about yourself, criticizing yourself, doubting yourself, even shaming yourself, you cannot truly be receiving God's Word for yourself. How we treat ourselves on the inside does show up on the outside. We must not become confused by our ability to separate what we say from what we feel or think. Have you ever said "I am okay" when you are not okay? Do you want to know why they asked you if you were okay? Because you didn't look okay. What is going on on the inside rises to the surface in all of us.

Have you ever encountered an angry usher on the welcoming committee? The title and position may say one thing, yet what you encountered was a whole other thing. It is not enough to pretend you are who you want to be or have what you want to have. You must search to live your peace, your joy, and your freedom that God gave you. This starts by aligning your innermost thoughts with the truth God says that you are. Get rid of the negativity and deathly thoughts and replace them with the Word of life. It is time for you to choose.

Questions to Ask Yourself

1. What thoughts and attitudes do you have that tear you down?

2. Find a scripture for each one of them to contradict it and empower you. There are some in the back of the book to help you get started. Make note cards or post them where you can see them

3. Every time you think or say the negative thing, use your scripture to replace it by speaking it to yourself and stand firm on it to believe it to be true. (Speak it out loud, even if only a whisper. Life and death are in your tongue. So give yourself life.)

4. This process is a forever process. Thoughts, words, past moments will come, but it is up to you to use your sword to cut the head off of that thing.

5. Sharpen your sword and cut it down! You do this by using the Word of God coupled with faith. Whether you have one word or many, only your belief in them will change the results, attitudes, and quality of your life.

Pray This Prayer with Me

Father, Thank You for your Word that gives me light into who I am in You and who You created me to be. I commit to surrendering daily my thought processes that contradict Your Word and purpose in my life. Lord, Thank You for loving me even when I have not been kind or loving to myself. This day I choose to believe and trust in You. I love You, Lord. In Jesus' name, amen.

CHAPTER 10

Family Tree

I have always wanted to know where other peoples' actions, behavior, and attitudes come from. What we see on the surface is never what truly lies beneath. We tend to judge the fruit without understanding or considering the seed in which it came from. For example, a lot of promiscuous girls/women are so because they have been molested, sexually assaulted, disrespected, or verbally abused. They have come to believe this is all there is, and their value is tied up in it as well. But today we need to venture beyond our portion into the seed of our ancestors. Even their actions (fruits) are tied to the seeds deep within.

The spirit of fear can be a generational curse. What I mean by that is it very well could have attached itself to your ancestors a long time ago. The same fear I have been struggling with is the same fear that my parents have and what I can now see in my children. We may realize it and even attempt to swing at it, but our relationship with it keeps us from taking that final blow. We can, without question, get up to bat for someone else and hit a home run, but when it comes to ourselves, we may waiver in our timing and belief in who we are and whether we can actually do it. Fear keeps us from our own victories, and a lot of the time this leaves us to find victory through other people's triumphs, which still leaves a longing for our own.

Digging up the seed requires you to pull up and throw out ancient thoughts and hang-ups as well. My parents are amazing encouragers, but since they have had their own battle with fear, they have spoken negatively about their own lives without even realizing it. They were conditioned to seeing or hearing certain things and applying their own words instead of God's Word to it. In no way am I putting them down. I adore them and know that I was handpicked by God for them, but we need to understand how this spirit likes to attach itself not only to us, but to our legacy of greatness.

Here is an example: One day I was having a conversation with my dad while standing beside his bus in a parking lot. We were talking about traveling and he kept saying where he would not go out of the States. (Pretty much everywhere.) Now some may say to me "Neither would I," but it was in that moment it hit me. Although he has been in every part of the USA and on many cruises, taking a direct flight out of the country was not an option. It was very "old school" to believe if you fly to another place you may never come home, so just don't do it. He had always talked about seeing other places, but fear had kept him from going the distance. So many memories came rushing back to me on how fear had been operating in many different areas of his life. Even the memories of his childhood he had shared with us throughout the years were laced with fear. It was as if fear had been hiding right there next to him all along, but now it was in plain sight because I was aware of its presence. It was in this very moment this problem, this addiction, this spirit of fear was being seen as the parasite it truly is and how its infectious being can be passed on from generation to generation.

So I began to pray for revelation and for God to open my eyes to not only what I thought I was dealing with but what I was looking for, for my entire family. I ran through my life and my parent's lives and their parents' lives, and there it was over and over again. You see, if fear can stop one generation from succeeding in their purpose and keep them from prospering, it will look to chain them to their present while stealing away their future. It will continue to take from the generations to come as well.

This is where it gets serious. This is where you and I realize disguising your addiction to fear doesn't work. No matter what you say to those around you, your children, or those you mentor, it will not go away but instead it will cross-pollinate unless you grab hold of it and get rid of it for real. Fear never just wants you! It wants everyone connected to you also.

The seed, the original intent, that kind of disease, is what is in your household. What kept your grandmother, great-grandmother, your father, your mother bound to their addiction? You don't just have to find it; you have to destroy its hold on you and your family, even the words attached to it. You must tear them straight out of your own mouth.

I won't allow anyone, not even my parents, to speak from a place of fear in my presence because I know that it feeds it and gives it strength. We cannot and should not allow our mouths or the mouths of others to speak death over our lives, thoughts, visions, purpose, dreams, and the lives of those around us. Death? Yes, death. Fearful words become death to whatever you are speaking them over. You are now aware and responsible. I am a visual person, so I imagine things into real situations, so imagine fear as a terrorist. This terrorist is cunning. It sets you up silently as it builds a way to terrorize you and intimidate you in your thoughts. Then it slithers away as if it had nothing to do with it.

How? Fear is like a terrorist that puts gasoline all over your house then hands you the lighters. No one realized he was a terrorist because he had been coming around for so long; he just seemed regular. The lighters he gave out looked really cool. They had different designs to match everyone's personalities, and although the house smelled funny, the temptation to flip the switch kept rising. Somehow a spark turned into a flame and the next thing you know, the house is gone, you feel terrible, and fear is whispering, "Oh no, what happened? You should have been more careful." You see, it seems to be helpful pretending to give wisdom after the fact without you realizing it was what sabotaged you in the first place. All of the things that have been set up around you, in you, and against you are waiting for your words to align with them to make the flames that try to destroy you.

Recognize the rat and don't play with his cheese. Just get rid of him and watch what you say. If you keep yourself covered in godly wisdom, you will be less likely to fall to fear's games. You must be alert of the harm you can do to yourself by not paying attention.

Questions to Ask Yourself

1. Where did the seed come from in your family?

2. Who else is suffering from the same addiction?

3. Don't confront them; pray for them.

4. Find all the negative, fearful words people use around you and over you and refuse to allow them to speak it ever again in your presence. Don't speak them either.

Pray This Prayer with Me

Lord, Thank You for the revelation of the seed of fear. Thank You that we are able to not only take it out of us but also those before us and those who come after us by Your words, our prayers, revelation, Your wisdom and Your deliverance power. Forgive me for every time I set a light to my own situation because of my lack of faith and relationship to fear. I Thank You for Your grace, forgiveness, love, peace, and mercy that You have given freely to all of us. I love You, Lord. In Jesus' name, amen.

CHAPTER 11

Do You Trust Me?

"You don't trust me?" God said to me clear as day while out on one of my walks. I was so hurt by this statement/declaration. "Of course, I trust you, Lord, I love you," I replied. "No," the Lord replied and went on to tell me why.

"When you ask for something concerning your children, you don't wait for my response. You start deciding what to do in your own might before you even finish your request. Most of your prayers already have four fallout plans just in case I (the Lord) may not answer or answer as you choose for me to."

As more examples came flooding in, I realized it was true. I loved God. I tried to be faithful, I even knew He could do what He chooses to. But did I believe He would? Did I believe it would come quick, or did I even deserve to ask for anything with all my past mistakes? I mean, who would blame God for not answering me or choosing to be done with me? Not I, I couldn't blame him at all.

I would pray, pray, and pray, then seal it with my favorite doubt phrase: "If it is your will." Which decoded means "If you don't answer me, Lord, it is okay, I wasn't sure about it anyway." We have a way of putting God and our "faith" in our prayers while removing them at the same time. Our lack of trust and fear of being disappointed leads us to be one foot in and one foot out all at the same time. We really didn't trust, believe, or have faith that He would have answered us.

Do you know how to trust? What I learned is, it wasn't that I didn't want to trust, but I didn't know how. With disappointments, ups and downs, and sharp turns, I hadn't developed true trust in anything or anyone. This is why control seemed to be my favorite tool of choice.

How can you trust God when you have no idea how to trust at all? It is a processes. God builds our faith in Him through our relationship with Him. Building your belief that you are never alone or forsaken is taking it step by step to build up your understanding and ultimate foundation on how to trust.

Questions to Ask Yourself

1. Do you have an issue with trust?

2. How do you think it plays out in your relationship with God?

3. How does it play out in your relationships with other people?

Pray This Prayer with Me

Father, teach me how to trust You and forgive me for every moment I did not trust You. I lay bare before You, waiting for your answer, direction, and guidance. Guide me in the paths of righteousness for your name's sake. I surrender to You in the name of Jesus, amen.

CHAPTER 12

Face Your Fears

Now that we have dug through to the back of the closet, so to speak, what do we do with all the stuff we have on the floor? I'm so glad you asked. The knowing is half the battle, but realizing, understanding, and grasping the process takes time, patience, grit, and most of all follow through. A.k.a., *action!* But remember, Rome was not built in a day.

It is time to set some small goals and test out some different methods of thinking and dealing with fear. You will be able to see clearer where fear and wisdom divide. So choose one to conquer and let me tell you how to start.

After the Lord told me I didn't trust Him, I came up with a strategy of how to start to learn. (May sound silly, but everything must start from something.) I needed to start with a plan that was more like a big wheel and less like a motorcycle. Something that kept me low to the ground and from freaking out. I decided to use my way to work. You see, fear takes center stage if you don't know the voice of God or how He operates. We must learn His ways so we can submit to them.

So there I was every morning, asking God which way I should go to work. Some days I'd hear or feel the Lord sending me out to the right from my street and some days to the left. Some days I would listen and other days I would intentionally go the opposite way. Every time I went in the direction I was led to, I wouldn't just show up on time, I would get there early. While every time I went the opposite of what I heard or felt, I was late. God never sent me the exact same way. But every time I went away from his direction, I ran into traffic.

I know, what does traffic have to do with my fear and anxiety? Nothing! I wasn't learning traffic tricks; I was learning to follow the direction of the Lord and trust in His guidance in my life. I needed to build confidence in what I was hearing and feeling and the directions I was given.

Now here is the disclaimer: Hearing from Him *is not* searching for an audible voice. It's understanding his character and ways. Not everyone will hear, see, smell, or so on. But everyone can judge their own growth in their relationship with God by their likeness to his character. I was reading my word, worshipping, meditating on His Word, and even spending time soaking (in silence) apart from my driving journey. God is not a god of tricks and magic. I was building a relationship with Him outside of asking directions. You must have and build a relationship of intimacy with the Lord to even begin to be sure you are hearing from Him and not any other spirit. *Do not skip out on spending time and investing in your relationship with Him!*

People believe that because God is God, we automatically know how to trust Him. Not so. If we don't trust, we must learn how. If we don't trust at all, we must start with a mustard seed of faith and not be ashamed that it isn't a full-grown tree.

In order to truly use your sword (Word of God), you have to have a trusting relationship with the one who created it. Reciting a word out of the Bible will be just that if there is no trust or relationship behind the words you say. God is faithful to do what he says He will do, but we can block our reception of His promise if we have no faith to receive it.

Having your word without any faith is like showing your enemy your sword and just leaving it in the holder. The Word is active, sharper than a double-edged sword, tears down strongholds, and is prophetic. Faith and fear are both action words. You are either putting one to work or the other. Are you swinging your sword? Are you confronting your fear? Be honest because He knows the truth. What does He see that others can't see in you?

Questions to Ask Yourself

1. What is your strategy?

   Pray, meditate, and believe He will meet you where you are.

   Remember: Make sure you are not just listening to any kind of spirit by staying prayed up and studying your word. Align what you hear, think, or even feel with the Word of God. He won't go against his own nature. Don't go it alone. God must be in it.

Pray This Prayer with Me

Lord, I pray today for a level of boldness like never before to begin to trust You from the innermost part of me. Teach me how to trust You, for You said, "You are the author and finisher of my faith." I need You, Lord. In Jesus' name, amen.

CHAPTER 13

Anger Is Not a Sin

That, however, is not the way of life you learned when you heard about Christ and were taught in him in accordance with the truth that is in Jesus. You were taught, with regard to your former way of life, to put off your old self, which is being corrupted by its deceitful desires; to be made new in the attitude of your minds; and to put on the new self, created to be like God in true righteousness and holiness. Therefore each of you must put off falsehood and speak truthfully to your neighbor, for we are all members of one body. "In your anger do not sin" Do not let the sun go down while you are still angry, and do not give the devil a foothold.

—Ephesians 4: 20–27

You have the right to be angry, just not the right to sin. Too often, we as a people deny our true feelings. Something happens and the first thing we say is "I'm okay." Even my grandbabies do it. But it is only moments later we see the effects of the fall. This is a learned behavior. Like when a young child falls and we clap and shout "Yay, you are okay." They are confused because they are not okay, but all of their guidance has encouraged them that they are. No, we do not want them to lay down and cry over every small thing, but we do want them to express their truth.

This is especially brutal in boys. Shake it off; take a salt tablet; you're a man, you are fine; boys don't cry; and so on and so on. My heart goes out to our brothers as they have been taught to deny their emotions and feelings altogether.

I have twin grandchildren, Avryanna and Zyair. We were blessed right out of the gate with one of each, a girl and a boy. It is in these two we can find clarity in how the sexes are defined so differently. Although they are equally loved and spoiled by everyone, it is clear who the boy is and who the girl is, especially by the men in the family. They are gentle with my granddaughter Avryanna, as she has all of them wrapped around her tiny finger, while my grandson Zyair, lovingly known as "Big Fella," is encouraged to get up when he falls down. Like I said, the love is the same, but the handling is different.

If we are not teaching our children, especially our boys, how to appropriately express themselves emotionally, we are stunting their thought process and relationship growth. We are teaching them how not to process pain. For example, there are five stages of grief, yet we find many people are told to not cry at funerals, but tears come with several emotions and feelings associated with grief. If there are five stages and tears are a part of their grieving process, we are training them how not to process their grief. The fact that we stifle ourselves and do not allow ourselves to be earnest and honest with the way we feel, keeps us from allowing God the space to heal us in our innermost being.

Anger is a byproduct of hurt, and hurt is a product of a trespass (whether intended or not). When we act out of anger without acknowledging it is hurt or its origin, we miss a great opportunity to heal. We have taken off layers, dug up not only our own past but our ancestors, and we have discovered things that were hidden seeds, roots, and fruit.

Anger comes in with a flood of frustration. It is easier to be angry than it is to be hurt. It's easier to find a bubble to stay numb inside of than to deal with what is or has been done to us. You may find yourself going through a rush of emotions. Don't stop them, define them. Dig deep into their roots and allow yourself to be upset with your past.

God knows we will deal with anger and all types of emotions. He even knows we may get angry with Him. It is not your anger He can't deal with; it's your unwillingness to be honest with Him about it. So share it with Him.

A friend of mine lost her mom while she (my friend) was expecting. Everyone throughout the planning and the funeral kept telling her she shouldn't be angry. Well, that made her worse. You could see the anger mounting into rage. She was angry with God for taking her mom, especially while she was expecting. She wanted her mother desperately in every way possible. Her pain felt unbearable.

While at the repass, I saw she was finally alone, so I went over and kneeled down next to her ever so gently. I whispered, "It's okay to be angry with God, He can take it. Just be honest with Him about where you are and eventually you will find your way back out. He can work with your honesty." She looked up at me. First in shock, and then relieved. We have the right to our feelings; we just don't have the right to be belligerent, disrespectful, or hurtful. So let yourself feel what you are feeling so one day you won't have to feel it anymore.

Questions to Ask Yourself

1. What are you feeling?

2. What is the true source of that feeling?

3. What part did you play in it if any? (Include blaming yourself or holding on to it with shame.)

4. Pray the Lord deal with it and for His peace in the process as you surrender it to Him daily.

5. Repent for your part.

Pray This Prayer with Me

Father, I'm hurting, I'm angry, I'm frustrated and aggravated. I don't want to be this way, but it is what I have today. Help me, God, to wade through each emotion so I can expose the source. Help me to speak my truth so that I can be free from its grasp. Lord, I've even been angry with You. Forgive me, Lord. I repent for any and every moment that I let my anger stand in the way of being obedient to You or that has kept me from You. I need You, Lord. Heal me from the brokenness in my heart. I surrender myself to You. In Jesus' name, amen.

CHAPTER 14

In My Daddy's Arms

The hardest thing about this journey isn't digging up the root issue or even exposing the infection; it isn't in the tears shed or even in the frustration and anger. No, it's in learning to let God love you. *What?* I know that may sound weird to some of you. But take a look at your reaction to these statements. God loves me even though He knows I still fail Him. God loves the naturally naked physical, emotional, and spiritual me. Even with all my shortcomings, God still loves me. How do these statements make you feel? Do they bring about some doubts, or do you want to run away from the thought of being totally exposed? How do you feel? Some of us truly have a difficult time receiving love or anything from others as well.

Most of us will say God loves me out of what we have learned or heard. But how many of us truly allow ourselves to sit in the Father's lap? I am a giver, but receiving was something I had to learn. My need to control (fear) kept me from allowing people to help me. Why? Because if they rejected me, or didn't do exactly what I needed, I couldn't be disappointed because I didn't let them in. (Yup, let them, as in let them help.) The same walls we build for others are the same walls that hold us from the fullness of God's love.

We think, *What if God decided He doesn't want to be a part of my life? What would that do to me?* But ask yourself, what if he wants to hold you like a loving parent holds their child? God's desire is to love on us in every way in every day. I am a mother of five and with each one of my children, labor was hard, but holding each one was an overwhelming love that I can't explain.

When a child is cradled in his/her father's arms, he/she can hear the comforting sound of their parent's heart. It's as if the rhythm is soothing. Even a fussy baby will calm down when they have been cradled and feel the warmth of that embrace.

Unfortunately, some children haven't had this amazing experience. Studies have shown that babies who had not been cradled and held had stunted growths. Even though these children are being fed, touch is still so important. Now let's take a look at our relationship with God.

We aren't infants in the natural, but in our relationship with the Father, we have to *allow* ourselves to be like an infant who needs to be and desires to be cradled by God our Father. We jump ahead to learning his ways, seeking His face, bowing at His feet, and seeking His hand. A true painful reality is without knowing how to seek His heart, we have lost a key foundation of our relationship with our Father.

Skin-to-skin is a term used after delivery when they put the newborn directly on the mother's chest, not to feed but so that they have skin-to-skin bonding time (intimacy). They encourage fathers to have these special moments with their new babies as well.

Beloved, you need some skin-to-skin time with God, a designated time to just lay down, close your eyes, and envision yourself in the Father's loving arms, listening to the beat of your daddy's heart, His smell, His tender touch and sweet voice. This is how you learn to let him love you. This is how you build upon that mustard seed of faith, through trust and belief in the Father. This is where you will realize, understand, and grasp that He truly will never leave you or forsake you. Taking time to just be and not do is so important in the trusting process.

I found that my favorite place is in my daddy's arms. I am able to laugh there and cry there and sometimes I just need a big hug. God is almighty, strong, all-knowing, all-loving, and everything good and perfect. Yes! He is also your Father. (Abba, one of God's names, meaning father/daddy.) So why is it we can accept His judgment to be true and the assignment that He has given but not his lap to rest in? It's because we don't allow Him to be daddy. Rest in the Lord today. Seek His heart and not His hand. Draw into an intimate loving relationship with Him and you will see not only your tears flow, but your strength will grow also.

Questions to Ask Yourself

1. Seek God's heart.

2. Lay down and envision laying in His arms.

3. Accept Him as your father, a loving and doting daddy.

4. Breathe, this is going to work.

5. Accept His love without serving, giving, worshipping, and so on.

6. This is you learning to be free.

Pray This Prayer with Me

Abba, I love you and today I put down my wall, so I can receive the love You have for me. Thank You for your open arms, green pastures, quiet waters, love, and peace. Cover me as only You can in your perfect peace. In Jesus' name, I Thank You and receive Your love. Amen.

CHAPTER 15

Wash Off the Dust because
Polish Makes Perfect

So you have a growing list of God's Word for you. This is awesome. Today you are going to choose one scripture reference that stands out to you the most and you are going to stay focused. Not the one with the most words. Not the one that seems the deepest or oh-so prophetic and sophisticated. No! No! Take the one that speaks to you the most. The one that jumps out to you at this very moment. The one that warms your heart. Remember, this is transformation. That takes time and consistency. It does not matter how long you have been "saved". In order to digest, trust, believe and receive the word, you must step back and chew one piece at a time.

I cannot recite the Bible word for word. (Don't close the book please.) But I know the love, peace, joy, strength, and unchanging hand of God. It is hard for me to retain everything at once, but I can and do receive and enjoy the Word of God and the life it gives me. My mom always tells the story of being in the adult Sunday school class when she first started going back to church. They became bothered with her "immature questions," so she said, "Whelp, this isn't the class for me. I need to know the basics and the foundations." And off she went to the children's church.

What I love about this moment is that she had no shame in wanting to know the foundations, so it could mean something to her. She decided not to stay in the adult class and learn how to speak about God, but instead she sought out how to receive Him in her heart. She desired a true relationship and not one on the surface for others to see.

Take that one scripture and don't just let it be your favorite verse; let it be your meal plan. Get filled up daily on that Word. Receive it in such a way to fill your spirit and edify your soul. Meditate on it, find its original meaning in each word, gain definitions of the main words, and truly digest each portion. Eat of it with joy, gladness, and a true expectation that it will become active in your life.

Questions to Ask Yourself

1. Find your scripture.

2. Work on believing that its truth is for you.

Pray This Prayer with Me

Father, we Thank You for the elementary things that feed us the most profound nourishment. Your Word not only speaks to us; it gives us power and strength. It tears down that which is not of You so that we can draw nearer to You. Thank You for Your words that are choice morsels that truly encourage my soul. I love You, Lord. In Jesus' name, amen.

CHAPTER 16

Learning to Breathe

This morning, during my time with the Lord, there were tears shed, pain released, questions answered, and newness to behold. At the end of it all, a deep breath closed it out. I couldn't remember the last time I took a deep breath. When is the last time you took a deep breath? A breath of release? A breath of peace? A breath that says "I have surrendered it all to you, God."

When dealing with fear, doubt, shame, and the need to control, we will find that most of our breaths are short and shallow. It is not often that we sit and take a few deep breaths, let alone live our days with consistent breaths of release and peace.

We find our chests are tight, our minds are racing, and overall our bodies are reacting to the stresses that so entangle us. Who has time to sit and just breathe, right? We rarely ever take a minute in the middle of the day to close our eyes and just consider breathing and focusing on the peace God offers. Instead we say "I can't do that," roll our eyes, clinch our hands, and tighten up more than we already have been.

I don't drink alcohol, and this is not a condemnation by any means; I realize that alcohol can relax you. But let's look at what you allow yourself to do in the moment you kick up your feet (so to speak) and pour a glass of wine. Do you not allow yourself to stop in that moment and take a breath? Do you not allow yourself to be still and press pause on life for a moment? Even if you are talking about why you need the glass so bad, aren't you allowing yourself to take a timeout and step out of the reality of it all to gain a new perspective or just take a breath? So couldn't it be that you do know how to stop and take a moment, a deep breath moment, when you normally say I don't have time for that? Don't get stuck on the glass of wine. Replace the glass of wine with what you use to relax instead of giving your stress to God.

My form of relaxation, release, or coping didn't come by wine; it was dredged in chocolate. Every moment I became overwhelmed, I would get my hands on some kind of chocolate to soothe my stress and/or pain. I have driven almost an hour one way just to get ice cream from a particular shop I love.

During one particular recital season, I was overly stressed. Every season is stressful. I had a candy bar next to me or I was stopping at a store consistently and daily. While speaking to a dear friend of mine on the phone, she demanded, "No more chocolate!" She told me to put the chocolate down, it was time to fast from it until after the recital. Mind you I had about a month to go.

I quickly ate the rest of what I had and agreed to the fast. I committed to giving God all of my stresses and woes, just as I should have been doing all along. This was me putting into practice Philippians 4:6–7: "Do not be anxious about anything, but in every situation, by prayer and petition, with thanksgiving, present your requests to God. And the peace of God, which transcends all understanding, will guard your hearts and your minds in Christ Jesus." You see, what we are truly searching for is peace in the midst of it all.

So if the Word says prayer (talking) and petition (formal request), present your request to God with thanksgiving, and the peace that surpasses (exceed/greater than) our understanding will guard your heart. We need to start breathing out our all to God. Don't hold back; He knows it all anyway. Speak it out, cry it out, yell it out, get it out, and give it all to Him. Don't be politically correct in prayer, be honest. The Word says Jesus is our friend. So why don't you allow yourself to have a real friend-to-friend conversation with Him? Be honest, open, and transparent.

You can't gain peace if you haven't shared your truth with God. But when you have, you can have peace anywhere and anytime. You won't have to wait for happy hour, a friend to answer your call, or anything else you seek to calm you down. Every minute, God is there to receive your request, hear your heart, and trade your concerns for the peace he has for you. So open up and breathe it out. Trust me, the world will not end while you are taking a moment to do so.

Questions to Ask Yourself

1. Today count how many times you take a deep breath.

2. Make a commitment to yourself to take more deep breaths daily.

Pray This Prayer with Me

Father, help me to breathe out the stresses that entangle me and the distractions that keep me from You and Your peace. Lord, I take a breath today and breathe You in. Thank You for listening to me and being concerned about me and loving me like you do. I surrender all of my anxieties (name them all) to You Thank you for handling them all on my behalf and giving me Your perfect peace. Thank You, God, for who You are and who You are in me. I love You with all I have. In Jesus' name, amen.

CHAPTER 17

I've Come This Far, What Now?

I know we have had so much meat and potatoes, so what now? In every journey, there is proper alignment. Whether it's just you and the Trinity (Father, Son, and Holy Spirit) or God sends you someone to be with you, we all need to be properly connected and aligned.

When Jesus was on earth, he showed us these connections and alignments. With his disciples, he had connections that he walked in daily. In Scripture, you see how he was aligned with the Godhead when he was recorded in prayer. He came to give us a daily living design, so don't miss it. Even when God created man, He said, "It is not good for man to be alone." Well, my love, you need someone to walk with you. Let me be very clear that this cannot be just anyone or that you should be the one who chooses this person. No, this is a prayer request opportunity. This will also be the opportunity to see who God chooses to move in and out of your life.

Many years ago, I went through a very difficult time in my life and I needed a few people to walk alongside me. Each one for a different portion of this particular season. Yes, it was a rough time and I needed a few people. They each played a different part but collectively were there for one purpose. Each one had come into my life briefly before or during my crisis, and as swiftly as they came into the season is as swiftly as they went out when the season was over. What am I saying? Don't worry about getting attached to each person; just consider getting the information you need for this season.

Although this is a very private and personal moment in your life, it is critical to have someone there to hold you up and keep you accountable. What I didn't allow myself to do is only surround myself with people who agreed with me. I needed someone to tell me if my stuff stinks.

Accountability is key in life. As much as we can say I'm responsible, I've got this. The truth is without accountability, we will fall short or run the risk of getting offtrack. Now if you're saying it's always been just me, let me remind you of the Trinity (Father, Son, and Holy Spirit); even God is working together. He created us to be in union with him and with each other. I have felt alone myself, many days unsure of my own choices in friends and confidants. What I learned is I had to stop choosing them and let God send them, that sometimes I was looking for others to be there when God was trying to have private moments with me.

Every one of us craves human interaction. So it's not whether we need it, it is the question of who's the right person for this job. Who will hold you accountable to the words that come out of your mouth? Who will keep you close to God's standards? Who will remind you that life and death are in the tongue so you should watch how you speak? Who will hold you to your commitment to your journey? Who will be there to support you and encourage you? Who? Let God decide.

Questions to Ask Yourself

1. Who will be your accountability partner/s?

2. Know what to share.

Even with accountability, there is wisdom to know what is only between you and God, you and your spouse (if you are married), and which part they are assigned to. For example, if you have an accountability partner for working out, this does not mean they are prepared, equipped, or sent by God to handle, deal with, impart wisdom, or even listen to your concerns about your deepest pain. Know what to share with whom and whether to share it if at all.

3. Allow yourself to take this step. This is huge, but a load shared is easier to carry. So take a breath and take the step.

4. Call them. Don't lose your nerve, call them, and set a time to meet. Make sure you commit to face time, not text, email, or social media. In no way is that personal. If your person happens to live far away, still try to use face time if possible, but at least let them hear your voice and you hear their voice.

Pray This Prayer with Me

Father, Thank You for always being with me. Even when I thought I was alone, You were there to cover me and guide me. I pray that my eyes and ears will be open to receive Your direction and that I walk in obedience to You. Father, send me the person or persons You would have to walk alongside me in this season. Make it so clear that there is no question that it is them. Help me to be clear on what to share with them and what to keep for our private time together. I Thank You for this exciting new step in my journey. I love You, Lord; Thank You for loving me. In Jesus' name, amen, amen, and amen.

Guiding Thoughts

Remember the final word is always God's. Do not get confused by this union. They're not to replace God, the Word, prayer, or time in devotion; they are to walk alongside you as needed, not to be your focus or crutch. You still go to God *first, foremost, and even after you have talked to the person.* If you have not prayed, then you should not make a call, text, email, post, or anything to them yet. Ask God first, tell God first, know the right position to be in. Keep proper perspective through your relationship and guidance from God.

CHAPTER 18

Maintaining Your Peace

As a dancer, I understand that our core is extremely important; except as a mother and teacher, I had let mine go. Even though on the outside it appeared my core was intact on the inside, it was not doing its job at all, which led to my two back surgeries. Since I have been dancing for most of my life, I could still turn, jump, leap, and so on, but I did notice that my core was not as strong as it should be. I had stopped training my body to stay strong.

When I was training as a young girl, the exercises and movements kept my core intact. But as I grew older, I hadn't been doing the work I still needed to maintain my body. The core keeps the body strong. If it is not functioning properly, all of our body parts can experience pain, discomfort, and all sorts of problems or injuries. So I'm sure you're asking, *What does this have to do with my peace?* Well, if you don't engage your peace, it will grow weaker and so will you. Peace helps us to think properly, maintain a calm state of being, enjoy moments, sleep, and so on.

Our peace comes with our ability to surrender our fears to God. I know I've used these words a lot and will continue to do so because not only is it key but it is life-changing. The thing we need to get into our everyday thoughts is if we are not engaging our peace through surrender, thanksgiving, and accepting that which God has freely given us, then we will find ourselves wavering over and over again and becoming weaker in our core (peace). Only when we seek Him with all our heart poured out will we see the manifestation of His peace that surpasses all understanding.

We often begin to feel some relief and lose sight of what got us there in the first place. Just like when the doctor tells you to finish all the medication they have prescribed, but you start to feel a little better and stop taking it. When we don't finish it, we run the risk of getting worse or staying the same. It is important to continue to do the thing that brought you the results you first desired. The aim is healing and release of pain and suffering.

Your peace is something you maintain through your daily exercise of prayer. Imagine every day you have a large load of dirty clothes. You take it to the cleaners and they swap them out for new ones. If there are tears in them, they mend them if it is meant for you to keep them, but the ones that are of no use to you they just replace with something useful.

When we bring our anxieties to God with a thankful heart for our answered prayer requests, we receive the peace that comes with it. Peace that says, "I know God will handle it in His time and in His way, but in any case I'm okay because I trust Him." Peace that goes beyond what we could even pray for. Peace that guards our heart and minds in Christ Jesus. We don't have to walk around with dirty, torn, and dusty clothes on (a.k.a., anxiety, stressed out, worried hearts). Rather, we can be clothed in His peace, which will bring a filling of joy that brings strength to our soul. Peace is not the absence of troubles or difficulties; it's the presence of God in the midst of them that sustains us. It's knowing He is handling it in His time and His way and that we can trust Him with it all.

Peace is a currency exchange. What do I mean? Well, you have to give something over to get it in return, not to barter but to replace. If anxiety and fear are taking over your heart and mind, you must be willing to surrender them to gain Godly peace. This exchange empties out the space so peace can occupy it.

Make it your habit and build your core.

Questions to Ask Yourself

1. What haven't you surrendered to God that is holding your peace back?

2. Begin to surrender these things and thank God for caring about your concerns.

3. Make the transfer and pick up your peace.

Pray this Prayer with Me

Lord, today I stand grounded to maintain the peace You have set before me. I surrender all of my anxious thoughts to You and request that You take over them now and guide me in Your ways of righteousness. I Thank You for seeing me and answering my prayers, for You alone are worthy to be praised. I am so grateful for the peace that You have given me to guard my heart and mind. I love You, Lord, in Jesus' name, amen.

CHAPTER 19

Can you Walk and Talk?

In the last chapter we discussed your peace through your prayer life. Today I want to do your walk and talk with God/ your Father.

Too often we leave prayer to our prayer closets, pulpits, prayer lines and the intercessors. But if God is with you wherever you are why do you only talk to him when you get home? I am not suggesting designated or isolated prayer time isn't of great value in your relationship with your Father. Of Course it is. Rather I am saying that throughout your day you should spend time speaking with your Lord. With every other relationship in life you have to wait until the phone rings, they text, facetime and so on. But with your Heavenly Father you can speak to him at all times, any time of the day. There isn't a moment when God can't hear you so why save your conversation to a particular time. There is no separation unless you choose to remove yourself from him in your heart.

I have found in my journey some of the best moments and memories I have with the Lord in "prayer" are those that I spent laughing with him. God enjoys laughter. If your prayer life looks and sounds only like the King James Version of the bible, you are missing out on such a great opportunity to enjoy the laughter and sunshine smile of our Lord. The Trinity is a unity of love that courses through our veins, if we let it. So, let me ask you, when is the last time you laughed with your Heavenly Father?

Is it hard to imagine God as the daddy you can sit in his lap and giggle with? Does that seems far-fetched? The bible tells us the joy of the Lord is our strength. How can you increase in strength? By the joy of the Lord. How can you experience such joy? By spending time with him, engaging him in every situation and fostering an intimate relationship with him.

Of Course, there will be days you cry and feel sorrow, so didn't Jesus. Even his last moments in prayer were filled with blood mixed with sweat. There will be days of frustration and even anger but remember that joy comes in the morning. Sometimes your morning will come when you separate your mind from the moment you are in and look into the heart of God and inquire of the peace and joy he offers you. As we share our hearts with God throughout the day, about both great and not so great things, we will find that our heart becomes closer to his heart and his peace becomes our peace and his joy becomes our strength to endure. Take time to enjoy building a relationship with God. Trust me it is amazing.

Questions to Ask Yourself

1. Take today to speak with God about *everything,* even the silliest of things.

2. Record how it made you feel. Do it as often as you can and would like to.

Pray This Prayer with Me

Lord, Thank You for not only being God but my daddy, for desiring a relationship with me that has laughter built into it and peace abounding. I pray that in each moment, I give You praise and keep my eyes on You. Even in the midst of my tears, I come to You, praying You fill my heart with joy and laughter that I may draw strength from You. Starting today, I will take time all throughout my day to speak with You about all things. Thank You for blessing me, providing for me, and loving me as only You can. In Jesus' name, amen.

CHAPTER 20

Made for This

Every person—whether past, present, or future—was created with a purpose. We all have gifts, talents, an anointing and purpose that are specific to us. No two people are the exact same; even twins' reactions and desires in life are specific to them. It is time to see what you are made for.

I know it may seem odd to be discussing your purpose in a book about fear, but let us dissect that for just a moment. If the spirit of fear keeps you from doing things, keeps you from learning, keeps you from pressing to new levels, it ultimately keeps you from fulfilling your life's purpose. Its intention is to keep you distracted and dismayed so that you are unproductive. It is our job to be clear on who we are and what we were made for.

During this activity, I want you to stay focused on the nature of a thing, not the title. Too often, people get consumed with gaining a title instead of producing the attributes of the position. I know, I know, what does that mean? Let me give you an example: Some people see ministry as a goal. They think, *I can do that, it looks cool,* or even, *I would love if everyone listened to what I have to say.* Well, to minister means "to serve." So I would ask them, "Are you ready to serve the people?"

DO NOT GET HUNG UP ON A TITLE! Yup, I was yelling to be clear. Our purpose is in our doing not just in what others call us or even what we want to be called. Learn to do the work of your purpose in the capacity you have been given. If you have a passion to serve or help the homeless, find ways to do so, even if no one is looking. Put together other like-minded people with the same passion and get it done.

If you love reading and writing, then find your way to writing your own book if it is in your heart to do so or help people like me by reading through their books and giving them feedback and corrections. A dear friend of mine (thank you, Erica) took this book and read it through and sent it back to me with notes. She took her love of reading and the English language and helped press me through. She has no idea the level of relief she offered me just by doing what she loves to do. She also doesn't know I added this little tidbit after she read through it all.

It is of great importance that we engage with our purpose. Understanding who we are brings our value to the surface. It can keep us from falling back into a relationship with fear or any other bad habit or dysfunctional relationship. Putting our purpose to work gives us back our power. When we focus on the good in us, we can find our way to build a better future and seek healing from our past. Don't just skip through this assignment; dive right in and go beyond the questions to gain answers and directions. You can even look up spiritual gifts assessment tests to go a little deeper. But if you choose to, please make sure you follow up with a reputable person or institute to gain understanding for all the different gifts that may be listed.

You must learn who you are so that you can experience life through His eyes. Remember, you can know that God loves you, but never accept His love because you don't feel worthy or feel that you deserve it. You don't, but the great thing is He didn't ask you to. He asked you to believe in Him and walk according to His will (with His help). God desires for you to know who you are and what you can do in Him. Don't stand in the way of your future or your blessings. Find your purpose and activate it. Remember, everything is about movement, whether you are moving away from something, toward something, or even standing your ground. What action will you take?

Enjoy this moment. Be confident in the things you love and are passionate about. Give to others that which you desire for yourself. Know the limits of everything you do and hold up that standard. Now dig deep.

Oh, and one last thing: Just because you are good at something doesn't mean it's the thing you are meant to do in this season. Sometimes people will steer you toward what they believe your strength is, but you have got to feel it in your heart to press into it at this very moment. It could be true, but it doesn't mean it's a now. So don't feel bad about it. Just hold it in your pocket until it is time.

Questions to Ask Yourself

1. What are you most passionate about in life (top 10 things)?

2. What talents/gifts do you have (top 5 to 10)?

3. Do you currently operate in any of your talents, gifts, or passions?

4. What do you feel your purpose is?

5. If you are unsure, where do your passions, gifts, and talents lead you to if you look at them on a five-to-ten-year scale?

6. How can you serve others with what you have?

7. Do you have a goal plan?

8. If not, please make a goal plan for today, one-month, three-month, six-months, one-year, and five-year plans.

Guiding Thoughts

I started with a day because we have to learn to give ourselves credit for the small things so that we can begin to trust ourselves to move onto what we would consider greater. If you are dealing with depression or even suicidal thoughts, please give yourself credit for getting up and out of bed today because I understand that is a purpose fulfilled. (note: if you have not sought out help thus far, make it your purpose to seek help today. Mental health is important) With that said, ladies and gentlemen, don't beat yourself up. Life comes with unexpected challenges every day. It isn't our job to downgrade ourselves and push ourselves to the side. Dust yourself off, whether it's been a day, a week, a month, or a year and get back at it. This life isn't a sprint; it's a marathon. So keep pressing.

Check the definition of the things you have discovered. I have been teaching, ministering the Word, praying for my students and their families, counseling students and their families, pouring into them, answering questions, and giving guidance for years. It wasn't until I did a gifts assessment that I realized I had been pastoring for over ten years. Again, it wasn't about the title; it was about the heart to serve and gaining understanding of who God made me. Sometimes we don't realize we are already doing what God created us to do; we just aren't doing it in the "traditional" way or what we think or have learned it is supposed to look like. In other words, whatever you are meant to do doesn't need a title, it just needs for you to get it done.

Do it afraid. Do what you can with what you have. Just do it. While you are working on moving past your relationship with fear, you may just have to venture out and get things done while you are still afraid. Just don't stop pressing. And do what you can in the moment. Another pastor once asked me how our church of humble beginnings was doing so much outreach. I told him, "Whomever is willing and whatever we have we just get it done." Someday it will be on a larger scale and reach more people, but we aren't waiting for that day; we are getting things done today. So today we are able to feed twenty homeless people, and we will. One day we will be able to feed two hundred and that will be fine too. But for now, we are not waiting; we are being active with what we have and what we can do. Get active and stay active. Don't let size or distance stop you from moving forward. The only way to get upstairs is by taking that first step and all the ones in between. Just keep stepping.

Pray This Prayer with Me

Father, today is such an exciting day to look into Your designer eyes and see what You have placed in me. I pray that I will be honest with my answers so that I can get Your honest design for my life. Lord, for every part of me, I give You thanks. Thank You for creating road maps and others to help me on life's journey and the opportunity to live my life without fear but with an understanding of who I am. I Thank You. In Jesus' name, amen.

CHAPTER 21

My Journey Begins

This journey takes practice. Like an intervention, it has been the beginning of the understanding of where you are currently and the options set before you to make the necessary changes. These twenty chapters discuss the beginning of realigning your thoughts for transformation to a solid and clear way of thinking.

It may have taken you a few days on each chapter to process that chapter. That is okay. You will definitely need to go back over and over again as you tear down new layers and discover new revelations. I am so excited for the peace you will gain and the deep breaths you will experience as you submit to breaking the chains of fear that have kept you captive.

Each day, commit to this wholeheartedly, that you will continue to press forward even in the darkest hour. Continue to study, read, do your research, and investigate for your own learning, understanding, and wisdom processes. Set your mind on receiving your deliverance and don't give up. I repeat, *don't give up!* It is not an option. Be proud of yourself for taking this on and not dying with the chains of fear wrapped around you or connected to the ones you love. You are now a *chain breaker* and the buck stops here. Rejoice, be glad, be free, be filled with hope, joy, and peace for you are loved immeasurably and needed here on Earth more than you can imagine. Be blessed,

I leave you with this scripture that gives me peace, and I encourage you to picture yourself in this pasture of amazing green grass and a sweet-sounding brook.

> The Lord is my shepherd, I shall not be in want. He makes me lie down in green pastures, he leads me beside quiet water he restores my soul. He guides me in the paths of righteousness for his name sake. Even though I walk through the valley of the shadow of death, I will fear no evil, for you are with me, your rod and your staff, they comfort me. You prepare a table before me in the presence of my enemies. You anoint my head with oil; my cup overflows. Surely goodness and love will follow me all the days of my life, and I will dwell in the house of the Lord forever. (Psalm 23)

Pray This Prayer with Me

Today I commit myself to this journey of love, to receive it from You, and to have it for myself. Forgive me for every moment I did not show You love by not loving who I am in You. Forgive me for serving fear instead of You, Lord. I surrender my all to You today. Cleanse me and wash me anew. I love You, I Thank You, and I honor You, Father, for You alone are worthy of all the praise. Thank You for always loving me and never leaving me, for holding me up even when I could not see it, and keeping me covered when I fell down. Lord, You are awesome. In Jesus' name, I pray, hallelujah and amen.

SCRIPTURE REFERENCES

Please always take time to read above and below the scripture references. Gain more wisdom, revelation, and understanding by searching out the Word of God for yourself.

The Lord's Prayer

This, then, is how you should pray:
"Our Father in heaven,
hallowed be your name,
your kingdom come,
your will be done,
on earth as it is in heaven.
Give us today our daily bread. And forgive us our debts,
as we also have forgiven our debtors.
And lead us not into temptation,[a]
but deliver us from the evil one."
(Matthew 6:9–13)

You Were Created

So God created mankind in his own image, in the image of God he created them; male and female he created them.

God blessed them and said to them, "Be fruitful and increase in number; fill the earth and subdue it. Rule over the fish in the sea and the birds in the sky and over every living creature that moves on the ground."

Then God said, "I give you every seed-bearing plant on the face of the whole earth and every tree that has fruit with seed in it. They will be yours for food. And to all the beasts of the earth and all the birds in the sky and all the creatures that move along the ground—everything that has the breath of life in it—I give every green plant for food." And it was so. God saw all that he had made, and it was very good. And there was evening, and there was morning—the sixth day. (Genesis 1:27–31)

New Creation

Therefore, if anyone is in Christ, he is a new creation: the old has gone, the new is here! (2 Corinthians 5:17)

I have been crucified with Christ and I no longer live, but Christ lives in me. The life I now live in the body, I live by faith in the Son of God, who loved me and gave himself for me. (Galatians 2:20)

Who Are You?

If you fully obey the LORD your God and carefully follow all his commands I give you today, the LORD your God will set you high above all the nations on earth. All these blessings will come on you and accompany you if you obey the LORD your God:

You will be blessed in the city and blessed in the country.

The fruit of your womb will be blessed, and the crops of your land and the young of your livestock—the calves of your herds and the lambs of your flocks.

Your basket and your kneading trough will be blessed.

You will be blessed when you come in and blessed when you go out. The LORD will grant that the enemies who rise up against you will be defeated before you. They will come at you from one direction but flee from you in seven.

The LORD will send a blessing on your barns and on everything you put your hand to. The LORD your God will bless you in the land he is giving you.

The LORD will establish you as his holy people, as he promised you on oath, if you keep the commands of the LORD your God and walk in obedience to him. Then all the peoples on earth will see that you are called by the name of the LORD, and they will fear you. The LORD will grant you abundant prosperity—in the fruit of your womb, the young of your livestock and the crops of your ground—in the land he swore to your ancestors to give you.

The LORD will open the heavens, the store-house of his bounty, to send rain on your land in season and to bless all the work of your hands. You will lend to many nations but will borrow from none. The LORD will make you the head, not the tail. If you pay attention to the commands of the LORD your God that I give you this day and carefully follow them, you will always be at the top, never at the bottom. Do not turn aside from any of the commands I give you today, to the right or to the left, following other gods and serving them. (Deuteronomy 28:1–14)

what is mankind that you are mindful of them,
human beings that you care for them?
You have made them a little lower than the angels
and crowned them with glory and honor.
You made them rulers over the works of your
hands; you put everything under their feet:
(Psalm 8:4–6)

For you created my inmost being;
you knit me together in my mother's womb.
I praise you because I am fearfully and wonderfully made; your works are wonderful,
I know that full well.
My frame was not hidden from you
when I was made in the secret place,
when I was woven together in the depths of the earth.
Your eyes saw my unformed body;
all the days ordained for me were written in your
book before one of them came to be.
(Psalm 139:13–16)

"You are the salt of the earth. But if the salt loses its saltiness, how can it be made salty again? It is no longer good for anything, except to be thrown out and trampled underfoot. "You are the light of the world. A town built on a hill cannot be hidden. Neither do people light a lamp and put it under a bowl. Instead they put it on its stand, and it gives light to everyone in the house. In the same way, let your light shine before others, that they may see your good deeds and glorify your Father in heaven. (Matthew 5:13–16)

Now if we are children, then we are heirs—heirs of God and co-heirs with Christ, if indeed we share in his sufferings in order that we may also share in his glory. (Romans 8:17)

No, in all these things we are more than conquerors through him who loved us. (Romans 8:37)

For we are God's handiwork, created in Christ Jesus to do good works, which God prepared in advance for us to do. (Ephesians 2:10)

But you are a chosen people, a royal priesthood, a holy nation, God's special possession, that you may declare the praises of him who called you out of darkness into his wonderful light. (1 Peter 2:9)

My Purpose

But I have raised you up for this very purpose, that I might show you my power and that my name might be proclaimed in all the earth. (Exodus 9:16)

so is my word that goes out from my mouth:
It will not return to me empty, but will accomplish what I desire and achieve the purpose for which I sent it. (Isaiah 55:11)

For I know the plans I have for you," declares the LORD, "plans to prosper you and not to harm you, plans to give you hope and a future. Then you will call on me and come and pray to me, and I will listen to you. You will seek me and find me when you seek me with all your heart. (Jeremiah 29:11–13)

And we know that in all things God works for the good of those who love him, who have been called according to his purpose. For those God foreknew he also predestined to be conformed to the image of his Son, that he might be the first-born among many brothers and sisters. And those he predestined, he also called; those he called, he also justified; those he justified, he also glorified. (Romans 8:28–30)

There are different kinds of gifts, but the same Spirit distributes them. There are different kinds of service, but the same Lord. There are different kinds of working, but in all of them and in everyone it is the same God at work. (1 Corinthians 12:4–6)

Now you are the body of Christ, and each one of you is a part of it. And God has placed in the church first of all apostles, second prophets, third teachers, then miracles, then gifts of healing, of helping, of guidance, and of different kinds of tongues. Are all apostles? Are all prophets? Are all teachers? Do all work miracles? Do all have gifts of healing? Do all speak in tongues? Do all interpret? Now eagerly desire the greater gifts. (1 Corinthians 12:27–31)

Now the one who has fashioned us for this very purpose is God, who has given us the Spirit as a deposit, guaranteeing for what is to come. (2 Corinthians 5:5)

being confident of this, that he who began a good work in you will carry it on to completion until the day of Christ Jesus. (Philippians 1:6)

Freedom in Christ

So if the Son sets you free, you will be free indeed. (John 8:36)

It is for freedom that Christ has set us free. Stand firm, then, and do not let yourselves be burdened again by a yoke of slavery. (Galatians 5:1)

Love

Love is patient, love is kind. It does not envy, it does not boast, it is not proud. It does not dishonor others, it is not self-seeking, it is not easily angered, it keeps no record of wrongs. Love does not delight in evil but rejoices with the truth. It always protects, always trusts, always hopes, always perseveres. Love never fails. (1 Corinthians 13:4–8a)

And now these three remain: faith, hope and love. But the greatest of these is love. (1 Corinthians 13:13)

For in Christ Jesus neither circumcision nor uncircumcision has any value. The only thing that counts is faith expressing itself through love. (Galatians 5:6)

Forgive

Praise the Lord, O my soul, and forget not all his benefits [3] who forgives all your sins and heals all your diseases, who redeems your life from the pit and crowns you with love and compassion… (Psalm 103:2–4)

The LORD is compassionate and gracious, slow to anger, abounding in love. He will not always accuse, nor will he harbor his anger forever; he does not treat us as our sins deserve or repay us according to our iniquities. For as high as the heavens are above the earth, so great is his love for those who fear him; as far as the east is from the west, so far has he removed our transgressions from us. As a father has compassion on his children, so the LORD has compassion on those who fear him… (Psalm 103:8–13)

Who is a God like you, who pardons sin and forgives the transgression of the remnant of his inheritance? You do not stay angry forever but delight to show mercy. (Micah 7:18)

For if you forgive other people when they sin against you, your heavenly Father will also forgive you. (Matthew 6:14)

Strong and Courageous

Be strong and courageous. Do not be afraid or terrified because of them, for the LORD your God goes with you; he will never leave you nor forsake you." (Deuteronomy 31:6)

No one will be able to stand against you all the days of your life. As I was with Moses, so I will be with you; I will never leave you nor forsake you.

Be strong and courageous, because you will lead these people to inherit the land I swore to their ancestors to give them.

"Be strong and very courageous. Be careful to obey all the law my servant Moses gave you; do not turn from it to the right or to the left, that you may be successful wherever you go. Keep this Book of the Law always on your lips; meditate on it day and night, so that you may be careful to do everything written in it. Then you will be prosperous and successful. Have I not commanded you? Be strong and courageous. Do not be afraid; do not be discouraged, for the LORD your God will be with you wherever you go." (Joshua 1:5–9)

"Rise up; this matter is in your hands. We will support you, so take courage and do it." (Ezra 10:4)

Repent

From that time on Jesus began to preach, "Repent, for the kingdom of heaven has come near." (Matthew 4:17)

So watch yourselves.
"If your brother or sister□ sins against you, rebuke them; and if they repent, forgive them. (Luke 17:3)

Godly sorrow brings repentance that leads to salvation and leaves no regret, but worldly sorrow brings death. (2 Corinthians 7:10)

Where Do I Go and
How Will I Know You?

The LORD said, "Go out and stand on the mountain in the presence of the LORD, for the LORD is about to pass by."

Then a great and powerful wind tore the mountains apart and shattered the rocks before the LORD, but the LORD was not in the wind. After the wind there was an earthquake, but the LORD was not in the earthquake. After the earthquake came a fire, but the LORD was not in the fire. And after the fire came a gentle whisper. When Elijah heard it, he pulled his cloak over his face and went out and stood at the mouth of the cave.

Then a voice said to him, "What are you doing here, Elijah?" (1 Kings 19:11–13)

"Ask and it will be given to you; seek and you will find; knock and the door will be opened to you. For everyone who asks receives; the one who seeks finds; and to the one who knocks, the door will be opened.

"Which of you, if your son asks for bread, will give him a stone? Or if he asks for a fish, will give him a snake? If you, then, though you are evil, know how to give good gifts to your children, how much more will your Father in heaven give good gifts to those who ask him! So in everything, do to others what you would have them do to you, for this sums up the Law and the Prophets.

(Matthew 7:7–12)

Take my yoke upon you and learn from me, for I am gentle and humble in heart, and you will find rest for your souls. For my yoke is easy and my burden is light." (Matthew 11:29–30)

In that day you will no longer ask me anything. Very truly I tell you, my Father will give you whatever you ask in my name. (John 16:23)

Humble yourselves, therefore, under God's mighty hand, that he may lift you up in due time. Cast all your anxiety on him because he cares for you. (1 Peter 5:6–7)

This is the confidence we have in approaching God: that if we ask anything according to his will, he hears us. And if we know that he hears us—whatever we ask—we know that we have what we asked of him. (1 John 5:14–15)

We Need Him

Very truly I tell you, whoever believes in me will do the works I have been doing, and they will do even greater things than these, because I am going to the Father. (John 14:12)

"I am the true vine, and my Father is the gardener. He cuts off every branch in me that bears no fruit, while every branch that does bear fruit he prunes so that it will be even more fruitful. You are already clean because of the word I have spoken to you. Remain in me, as I also remain in you. No branch can bear fruit by itself; it must remain in the vine. Neither can you bear fruit unless you remain in me.

"I am the vine; you are the branches. If you remain in me and I in you, you will bear much fruit; apart from me you can do nothing." (John 15:1–5)

If you remain in me and my words remain in you, ask whatever you wish, and it will be done for you. (John 15:7)

For those who are led by the Spirit of God are the children of God. The Spirit you received does not make you slaves, so that you live in fear again; rather, the Spirit you received brought about your adoption to sonship. And by him we cry, *"Abba,* Father." The Spirit himself testifies with our spirit that we are God's children. Now if we are children, then we are heirs—heirs of God and co-heirs with Christ, if indeed we share in his sufferings in order that we may also share in his glory. (Romans 8:14–17)

Instructions

Then the LORD replied:
"Write down the revelation
and make it plain on tablets
so that a herald may run with it.
For the revelation awaits an appointed time;
it speaks of the end
and will not prove false.
Though it linger, wait for it;
it will certainly come
and will not delay. (Habakkuk 2:2–3)

All Scripture is God-breathed and is useful for teaching, rebuking, correcting and training in righteousness, so that the servant of God may be thoroughly equipped for every good work. (2 Timothy 3:16–17)

Where to Focus and Prepare

Those who guard their lips preserve their lives, but those who speak rashly will come to ruin. (Proverbs 13:3)

I consider that our present sufferings are not worth comparing with the glory that will be revealed in us. [19] For the creation waits in eager expectation for the children of God to be revealed. (Romans 8:18–19)

Do you not know that in a race all the runners run, but only one gets the prize? Run in such a way as to get the prize. Everyone who competes in the games goes into strict training. They do it to get a crown that will not last, but we do it to get a crown that will last forever. Therefore I do not run like someone running aimlessly; I do not fight like a boxer beating the air. No, I strike a blow to my body and make it my slave so that after I have preached to others, I myself will not be disqualified for the prize.
(1 Corinthians 9:24–27)

Since, then, you have been raised with Christ, set your hearts on things above, where Christ is, seated at the right hand of God. Set your minds on things above, not on earthly things. For you died, and your life is now hidden with Christ in God. When Christ, who is your life, appears, then you also will appear with him in glory. (Colossians 3:1–4)

For this reason I remind you to fan into flame the gift of God, which is in you through the laying on of my hands. (2 Timothy 1:6)

Hope and Renewed Strength

He gives strength to the weary
and increases the power of the weak.
Even youths grow tired and weary,
and young men stumble and fall;
but those who hope in the Lord
will renew their strength.

They will soar on wings like eagles;
they will run and not grow weary,
they will walk and not be faint. (Isaiah 40:29–31)

Yet you, LORD, are our Father.
We are the clay, you are the potter;
we are all the work of your hand. (Isaiah 64:8)

In the same way, the Spirit helps us in our weakness. We do not know what we ought to pray for, but the Spirit himself intercedes for us through wordless groans. And he who searches our hearts knows the mind of the Spirit, because the Spirit intercedes for God's people in accordance with the will of God. (Romans 8:26–27)

Not that I have already obtained all this, or have already arrived at my goal, but I press on to take hold of that for which Christ Jesus took hold of me. Brothers and sisters, I do not consider myself yet to have taken hold of it. But one thing I do: Forgetting what is behind and straining toward what is ahead, I press on toward the goal to win the prize for which God has called me heavenward in Christ Jesus. (Philippians 3:12–14)

Whatever you do, work at it with all your heart, as working for the Lord, not for human masters, since you know that you will receive an inheritance from the Lord as a reward. It is the Lord Christ you are serving. (Colossians 3:23–24)

Suit Up

The Armor of God
Finally, be strong in the Lord and in his mighty power. Put on the full armor of God, so that you can take your stand against the devil's

schemes. For our struggle is not against flesh and blood, but against the rulers, against the authorities, against the powers of this dark world and against the spiritual forces of evil in the heavenly realms. Therefore put on the full armor of God, so that when the day of evil comes, you may be able to stand your ground, and after you have done everything, to stand. Stand firm then, with the belt of truth buckled around your waist, with the breastplate of righteousness in place, and with your feet fitted with the readiness that comes from the gospel of peace. In addition to all this, take up the shield of faith, with which you can extinguish all the flaming arrows of the evil one. Take the helmet of salvation and the sword of the Spirit, which is the word of God. And pray in the Spirit on all occasions with all kinds of prayers and requests. With this in mind, be alert and always keep on praying for all the Lord's people. (Ephesians 6:10–18)

Prepare for Victory

no weapon forged against you will prevail, and you will refute every tongue that accuses you. This is the heritage of the servants of the Lord, and this is their vindication from me," declares the Lord. (Isaiah 54:17)

What, then, shall we say in response to these things? If God is for us, who can be against us? He who did not spare his own Son, but gave him up for us all—how will he not also, along with him, graciously give us all things? Who will bring any charge against those whom God has chosen? It is God who justifies. Who then is the one who condemns? No one. Christ Jesus who died—

more than that, who was raised to life—is at the right hand of God and is also interceding for us. Who shall separate us from the love of Christ? Shall trouble or hardship or persecution or famine or nakedness or danger or sword? As it is written: "For your sake we face death all day long; we are considered as sheep to be slaughtered."

No, in all these things we are more than conquerors through him who loved us. For I am convinced that neither death nor life, neither angels nor demons, neither the present nor the future, nor any powers, neither height nor depth, nor anything else in all creation, will be able to separate us from the love of God that is in Christ Jesus our Lord. (Romans 8:31–39)

For though we live in the world, we do not wage war as the world does. The weapons we fight with are not the weapons of the world. On the contrary, they have divine power to demolish strongholds. We demolish arguments and every pretension that sets itself up against the knowledge of God, and we take captive every thought to make it obedient to Christ. (2 Corinthians 10:3–5)

Finally, brothers and sisters, whatever is true, whatever is noble, whatever is right, whatever is pure, whatever is lovely, whatever is admirable— if anything is excellent or praiseworthy—think about such things. Whatever you have learned or received or heard from me, or seen in me—put it into practice. And the God of peace will be with you. (Philippians 4:8–9)

I can do all this through him who gives me strength. (Philippians 4:13)

Do Not Be Anxious Fear Can't Have You

You would think there would be more scriptures about fear. *But* fear is not as powerful as we make it. There is more power in knowing who you are and what you are called to be.

> Rejoice in the Lord always. I will say it again: Rejoice! Let your gentleness be evident to all. The Lord is near. Do not be anxious about anything, but in every situation, by prayer and petition, with thanksgiving, present your requests to God. And the peace of God, which transcends all understanding, will guard your hearts and your minds in Christ Jesus. (Philippians 4:4–7)

> For the Spirit God gave us does not make us timid, but gives us power, love and self-discipline. (2 Timothy 1:7)

> Humble yourselves, therefore, under God's mighty hand, that he may lift you up in due time. Cast all your anxiety on him because he cares for you. (1 Peter 5:6–7)

Wisdom

> The fear of the LORD is the beginning of knowledge, but fools despise wisdom and instruction. (Proverbs 1:7)

> Out in the open wisdom calls aloud,
> she raises her voice in the public square;
> on top of the wall she cries out,
> at the city gate she makes her speech:
> (Proverbs 1:20–21)

> Whoever gives heed to instruction prospers, and blessed is the one who trusts in the LORD. (Proverbs 16:20)

The one who gets wisdom loves life; the one who cherishes understanding will soon prosper. (Proverbs 19:8)

Encouragement

"Therefore I tell you, do not worry about your life, what you will eat or drink; or about your body, what you will wear. Is not life more than food, and the body more than clothes? Look at the birds of the air; they do not sow or reap or store away in barns, and yet your heavenly Father feeds them. Are you not much more valuable than they? Can any one of you by worrying add a single hour to your life? (Matthew 6:25–27)

But seek first his kingdom and his righteousness, and all these things will be given to you as well. Therefore do not worry about tomorrow, for tomorrow will worry about itself. Each day has enough trouble of its own. (Matthew 6:33–34)

We are hard pressed on every side, but not crushed; perplexed, but not in despair; persecuted, but not abandoned; struck down, but not destroyed. We always carry around in our body the death of Jesus, so that the life of Jesus may also be revealed in our body. (2 Corinthians 4:8–10)

Therefore we do not lose heart. Though outwardly we are wasting away, yet inwardly we are being renewed day by day. For our light and momentary troubles are achieving for us an eternal glory that far outweighs them all. So we fix our eyes not on what is seen, but on what is unseen, since what is seen is temporary, but what is unseen is eternal. (2 Corinthians 4:16–18)

Where Is Your Treasure?

"Do not store up for yourselves treasures on earth, where moths and vermin destroy, and where thieves break in and steal. But store up for yourselves treasures in heaven, where moths and vermin do not destroy, and where thieves do not break in and steal. For where your treasure is, there your heart will be also. (Matthew 6:19–21)

Covering in Times of Attack and Sleeplessness
**Put your name into this scripture and cover
yourself in it as you pray it over yourself:**

Whoever dwells in the shelter of the Most High
will rest in the shadow of the Almighty.
I will say of the LORD, "He is my refuge and my
fortress, my God, in whom I trust."
Surely he will save you
from the fowler's snare
and from the deadly pestilence.
He will cover you with his feathers,
and under his wings you will find refuge;
his faithfulness will be your shield and rampart.
You will not fear the terror of night,
nor the arrow that flies by day,
nor the pestilence that stalks in the darkness,
nor the plague that destroys at midday.
A thousand may fall at your side,
ten thousand at your right hand,
but it will not come near you.
You will only observe with your eyes
and see the punishment of the wicked.
If you say, "The LORD is my refuge,"
and you make the Most High your dwelling,
no harm will overtake you,
no disaster will come near your tent.

For he will command his angels concerning you
to guard you in all your ways;
they will lift you up in their hands,
so that you will not strike your foot against a stone.
You will tread on the lion and the cobra;
you will trample the great lion and the serpent.
"Because he loves me," says the LORD, "I will rescue
him; I will protect him, for he acknowledges my name.
He will call on me, and I will answer him;
I will be with him in trouble,
I will deliver him and honor him.
With long life I will satisfy him
and show him my salvation."

(Psalm 91)

CPSIA information can be obtained
at www.ICGtesting.com
Printed in the USA
LVHW010837280121
677609LV00006B/688

9 781098 034306